Contents

SAFETY ADVICE
When you make any of the projects in this book, always put safety first. Be extremely careful with sharp scissors, needles and pins and ask an adult if you need any help.

Learn stitches
Page 30

Slipper chic
Page 24

Eco Fashion

It's the new buzz word on the style scene, but what does eco-fashion really mean? Any fashion that takes into account the environment, the health of consumers (that's you!) and the working conditions of people employed in the fashion industry is part of the eco-fashion scene. And right now, that's the place to be!

Fashion and the environment

When buying new clothes or fashion accessories, look for ones made from eco-friendly raw materials. That means fabrics made from organic materials such as cotton that have been grown without the use of pesticides, and that have been coloured without the use of harmful bleaches or dyes. Also look out for clothes that make use of reused and reclaimed materials.

Make sure you save any pretty buttons or sequins from worn out clothes

4

CRAFTS
for
Styling your
Wardrobe

written by

Susannah Blake

WAYLAND

Published in paperback in 2013 by Wayland
Copyright © Wayland 2013

Wayland
338 Euston Road
London NW1 3BH

Wayland Australia
Hachette Children's Books
Level 17/207
Kent Street
Sydney, NSW 2000

Editors: Julia Adams; Katie Woolley
Craft stylist: Annalees Lim
Designer: Rocket Design
Photographer: Simon Pask, Ni Studios

The website addresses (URLs) included in this book
were valid at the time of going to press. However, it is
possible that contents or addresses may have changed
since the publication of this book. No responsibility for
any such changes can be accepted by either the author
or the Publisher.

British Library Cataloguing in Publication Data
Blake, Susannah.
   Crafts for styling your wardrobe. -- (Eco chic)
   1. Clothing and dress--Remaking--Juvenile literature.
   I. Title II. Series
   646.4-dc23

ISBN 978 0 7502 7853 9

Printed in China

10 9 8 7 6 5 4 3 2 1

Wayland is a division of Hachette Children's Books,
an Hachette UK company.
www.hachette.co.uk

Picture acknowledgements:
All step-by-step and craft photography:
Simon Pask, Ni Studios; images used throughout for
creative graphics: Shutterstock

Scarf sensation
Page 12

Reusable bag
Page 10

Create your own eco-fashion

Making your own trend statement by creating clothes and accessories out of reused, recycled, reclaimed and pre-loved materials instantly plants you firmly in the eco-fashion scene. Whether you're revamping an old jacket or cardigan with pretty ribbons and buttons or making a cool new scarf from scratch — as long as you're reusing, you're bang on trend!

Find your own inspiration

The secret behind really successful eco-styling is having an eye for the right materials. The first place to look is around the home, starting with your own wardrobe, then asking your family, friends and relatives. You can also check out second-hand clothes and accessories in charity shops.

Look out for fabrics and colours that you love. If clothes are worn out or too small, don't just throw them away. Snip off the buttons, save sequins, beads or ribbons, and hold on to knits. Even old blankets and curtains have the potential for turning into something fabulous!

Tie~d together belt

Use an old belt to make a new one! Remove the old buckle from a belt and attach it to a gorgeous new strap made from silky ties. You can even use the belt strap for another project, such as a strap for a new handbag!

2 Lay the ties on top of each other and feed the slim ends through the belt buckle.

1 Remove the strap from the belt buckle. Keep the belt buckle for this project and save the strap for a future project.

How to remove a belt buckle

A fabric or fake leather belt strap can be cut off using a pair of scissors. A leather belt strap may be attached with a popper, stud or stitching. For a stud, you will need to ask an adult to help you prise the stud open. If the belt is stitched, snip and unpick the stitches using a small pair of pointed scissors.

Leather belts can be tough, so take care when cutting them.

3 Use a running stitch (page 30) to hold the buckle in place.

4

Plait the ties.

Why stop at just one belt? You could make a range of belts to complement your wardrobe.

5

Sew the ends of the ties together with a pretty button. Use the gaps in the plaited strap to fasten the buckle in place around your waist.

This belt would work just as well tied around your favourite dress.

Reusable bag

You will need

★ heavy fabric, such as canvas, corduroy or denim
★ scissors
★ needle and thread
★ felt in various colours
★ buttons

Instead of using a plastic bag when you go shopping, always make sure you've got this handy pack-away bag tucked into your handbag. It's cool, gorgeous and good for the environment – and with eco-style in mind, it's only going to add to your fashion cred!

2

We chose to decorate our bag with leaves and flowers. For the flowers, cut out rounded crosses from the felt (see below), and pinch them together in the centre. Sew the pinched felt together.

1

Cut two 30 cm x 45 cm rectangles from the heavy fabric. Cut two long strips, 60 cm x 10 cm, from the same fabric.

Flowers and leaves look great in felt, but you could use hearts, butterflies or stars, too.

Drastic plastic

The average plastic bag is used for just five minutes, but takes about 500 years to decompose. Billions are used every year and end up littering streets and parks as well as pointlessly filling landfill sites. Plastic bags are dangerous, too, as they can kill birds and small mammals.

3

Once you have created your decorations, sew them onto one of the fabric rectangles. We used buttons to attach the flowers.

4

Turn the fabric with the decorations on its face and place it onto the other rectangle. Sew the rectangles together along three edges, leaving one short edge open.

5

Fold both long strips in half, lengthwise. Sew along the edges, leaving one short edge open. Then turn the fabric inside out. These will form the handles of the bag.

6

Fold back the open edges of the rectangles and sew them, creating a hem. Turn the rectangles inside out and sew the ends of the handles to the hemmed edges.

Your bag is ready for its first shopping trip!

Mac makeover

Upcycle your drab old winter mac or coat and turn it into something fabulous using scraps of old ribbon and home-made paper beads.

1

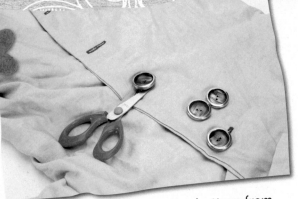

Remove any boring or broken buttons from the mac, and remove the belt if it has one.

2

Tear the tissue paper into small pieces and soak in water for about one hour, until very soft. Squeeze out most of the water, then mix in just enough PVA glue to make a thick paste. Shape the pulp into buttons and make two holes into the centre of them, using a bamboo skewer.

3

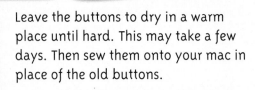

Leave the buttons to dry in a warm place until hard. This may take a few days. Then sew them onto your mac in place of the old buttons.

If you don't have any coloured tissue paper, make plain butons and paint them when they have dried.

4

Sew strips of fabric or ribbon onto the collars, cuff and pockets to make a smart trim. You can use the same ribbon or fabric as a belt.

5

Make a cute brooch for your upcycled mac by cutting out shapes from the felt. You can layer the shapes and create a trim using a blanket stitch (page 31). Sew the shapes onto your mac using pretty buttons.

Recycling ribbons

Silky ribbons are perfect for this project. You'll find them in all kinds of places – from gift wrapping and chocolate boxes to packaging for cosmetics. Keep your eyes peeled and always save any scraps you find so you've got a great selection to choose from.

Wow! How lovely does this fab 'new' mac look?

Scarf sensation

Getting woolly

If you know a knitter, ask them for any old balls of leftover wool they may have, or check out your local charity shop. Alternatively, unravel an old jumper or scarf. The wool will have lots of kinks and bends that will add to the fascinating texture of your pom poms!

Why make do with a boring old knitted scarf when you could have this fantastic fluffy pom pom scarf instead! Make it using leftover wool from a knitting project or reclaimed wool from an old jumper. Card from a cereal box is perfect for making the pom poms.

You will need

★ pencil
★ card
★ scissors
★ wool in different colours
★ compass
★ needle

1 Using a compass, draw two circles with a diameter of 9 cm. Then draw another circle inside each round with a diameter of 5 cm. Cut each of these rings out.

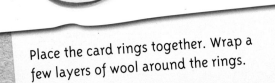

2 Place the card rings together. Wrap a few layers of wool around the rings.

3

Carefully snip around the outside of the rings, cutting through the wool loops.

4

Tie a length of wool between the two card rings to secure the wool loops. Tie the wool length in a tight knot and remove the card rings to reveal a fluffy wool pom pom.

5

Make at least 15 pom poms. Then, using a needle, thread them onto a long length of plaited wool to create your scarf.

Wool comes from animals such as sheep or alpacas. The animals are sheared, and the fleece is then cleaned and spun into the threads we use to make clothes.

Gilet glamour

Get the festival vibe with this stylish boho gilet! All you need is an old cardigan, some funky buttons and beads, and wool to create a tassled fringe.

2 Cut 7 cm lengths of wool. Fold a length in two, then poke the loop through a hole in the knitting around the arm hole. Tuck the cut ends through the loop and pull tight to produce a tassel.

1 Cut the sleeves off the cardigan about 2 cm from the seam, then fray the edges by cutting into them with a pair of scissors. Snip off any old buttons.

Broken beads

There's nothing so disappointing as breaking a favourite necklace and watching the beads roll away and get lost. But don't despair! Hold on to the remaining beads and use them in a project like this one. That way you can carry on enjoying your favourite necklace... even though it's not a necklace anymore!

3

Sew the new buttons onto the cardigan.

4

Using a tapestry needle and wool, sew beads onto the hems of the cardigan pockets. Use a whipping stitch (see page 31), threading a bead on with every stitch.

5

Sew strings of beads and bead tassles around the hem of the gillet to create a boho-style finish.

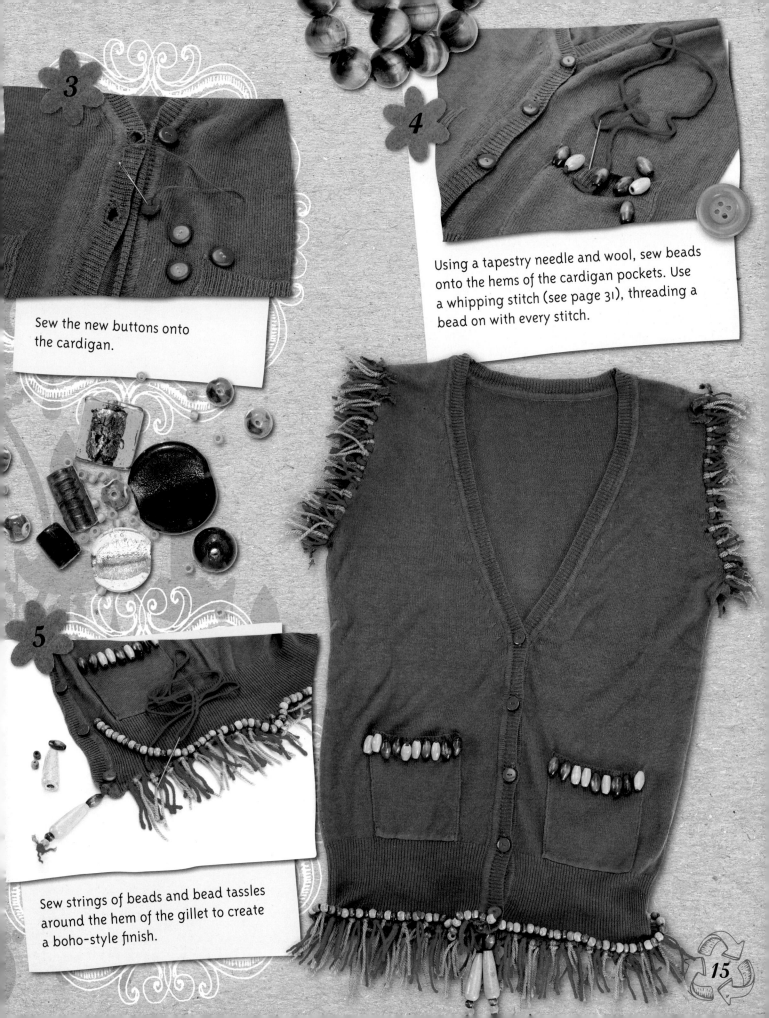

Perfect poncho

You will need

★ blanket or large piece of thick fabric
★ thread and wool
★ beads and sequins
★ needle
★ scissors
★ buttons

This South American classic is a great alternative to a conventional coat. Not only is it bang on trend, it's incredibly easy to make using an old blanket, decorated with embroidery and a beaded fringe. Save beads from old or broken necklaces and re-thread them to create your poncho decorations.

2

Fold two corners of the blanket together to make a triangle shape. Then snip a 'T' shape (approximately 20 cm long) in the centre for your head to go through. Use thread or wool to sew around the edges in blanket stitch.

1

Cut the blanket into a 1 metre x 1 metre square. Use thread or wool to sew around the edges in blanket stitch (see page 30).

Make your own blanket

If you don't have a blanket to use for this project, make your own patchwork blanket. You can do this by sewing together squares of scrap fabric from old clothes.

3

Cut shapes out of felt and decorate them with sequins. You can sew around the edges of the shapes in blanket stitch. Sew them onto the poncho.

Why not try making a traditional poncho for fancy dress?

4

Thread beads on to lengths of wool to make 5 cm-long tassels. Sew them onto the corners of the poncho.

Traditional ponchos have been worn for many hundreds of years in South America.

5

Decorate the collar of your poncho by sewing on lots of pretty buttons.

Groovy shoes

Clean up a grubby old pair of canvas pumps and transform them into something new and fantastic by decorating with patterns and adding flash shoe laces!

You will need

★ canvas pumps
★ soap and scrubbing brush (optional)
★ acryllic paints
★ sticky tape
★ permanent marker pen
★ coloured ribbon

1

Clean up the canvas pumps using soap and a scrubbing brush. Remove the old laces. Using a pencil, sketch pictures and patterns to create a funky all-over design.

2

Cut two pieces of ribbon to the length of the old shoe laces. Wrap sticky tape around the ends to stop them fraying.

You could ask an adult to clean your old pumps in the washing machine instead of scrubbing them.

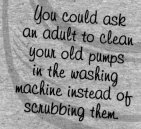

3

Fill in the shapes with the acryllic paint. Let the paint dry for a few hours.

Use a permanent marker pen to trace around the edges of the shapes. Then thread ribbons through the eyelets.

4

Share your shoes

About 330 million pairs of shoes are thrown out every year, ending up in landfill. Revamping a pair of shoes is a great way to chip away at this wastage. There are other ways you can help too. If shoes are too small, take them to a charity shop or recycling centre, so someone else can get some wear out of them.

Customising your shoes means that they are unique as well as eco chic!

Try using coloured insulation tape for the ends to add more colour.

19

Transform a T-shirt

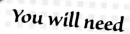
Bored of an old T-shirt and don't want to wear it any more? Give it a new lease of life by customising it in a few simple and fun steps!

1

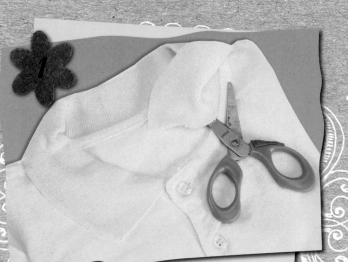

Use a pair of scissors to remove the collar.

2

Cut shapes out of the scrap fabric to create a cute motif. You can sew around the edges of the shapes in blanket stitch, too.

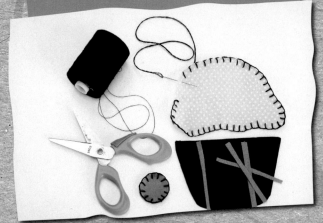

Unwanted clothes are often dumped in landfill sites.

3

Sew the shape onto the T-shirt and add buttons to decorate.

4

Cut thin strips of fabric and fold them like a concertina. Stick a needle and thread through each bundle of folded fabric.

Why not sew on your favourite cartoon character?

5

Pull the strips apart and sew them onto the hem of each sleeve.

A skirt to flirt!

Jazz up an ordinary skirt with a ruffled net petticoat and ribbon decorations to create the ultimate party piece!

1 Measure your waist, then double this measurement. Cut three strips of net curtain to this length and each strip as wide as the length of your skirt.

2 Sew the net ruffles to the underside of the skirt using a running stitch (page 30).

You can decorate your skirt with anything from sparkly brooches and sequins to fabric paints.

3

Cut thin strips of scrap fabric, as well as some pretty shapes with which to decorate the skirt.

4

Sew the end of a strip of fabric to the hem of the skirt; attach a second strip to it with a bow. Then sew on that strip and carry on attaching the strips until the hem of the skirt is decorated in a line of bows.

5

Sew the shapes you cut out earlier to the front of the skirt.

Slipper chic

You will need

- ★ cereal packet
- ★ pencil
- ★ an old fleece top
- ★ needle and thread
- ★ buttons
- ★ coloured felt

You can really make your own style statement with these cute and cosy slippers. Fleece from an old jumper or hoody is the ideal fabric and looks gorgeous decorated with reclaimed buttons.

1 Put one of your shoes on the opened out cereal packet and draw around it. Cut out the shape. Repeat with your other foot.

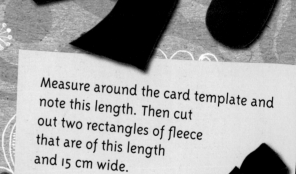

2 Place the card templates on the fleece and cut around them with a pair of scissors.

3 Measure around the card template and note this length. Then cut out two rectangles of fleece that are of this length and 15 cm wide.

Easy felt

Felt is a brilliant fabric for making slippers and you can make your own from an old jumper. Next time there's a hot wash going into the washing machine, throw in an old wool jumper that you don't wear any more. After a few hot washes you'll find that your old jumper has taken on a matted, felty texture that's perfect for turning into something new and funky.

4

Sew one fleece strip on to one of the fleece insoles, using a blanket stitch (see page 31) to make it really secure. Repeat with the second slipper.

5

To make the slipper shape, gather the front of the slipper by sewing around the top edge of the sides with a running stitch (see page 30).

Instead of buttons, you could attach pom poms to your slippers. Flip back to page 12 to see how to make them.

6

Pull the running stitch together to gather the front of your slipper and secure with a few stitches. You can sew a button onto the top to cover up the stitches.

Why not decorate the sides of your slippers with some pretty stars?

Dazzling jeans

You can bring a bit of sparkle to your old jeans by adding fabulous pocket patches, decorated with sequins and ribbons. Look out for sequins that you can snip off old clothes, and save those little pouches of spare sequins that often come attached to new sequinned clothes.

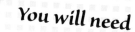

You will need
★ jeans
★ scissors
★ felt or fleece
★ needle and thread
★ sequins
★ ribbons

1 Cut a square out of felt that will fit onto your jeans back pocket.

2 Sew a decorative pattern on to the patch using sequins and ribbon.

You can even decorate your denim jacket with a few sparkly patches!

3

Sew the patch onto the jeans pocket with a whipping stitch (see page 31).

(see page 31)

Go organic

Growing cotton accounts for 25 per cent of the agro-chemicals used in the world. Denim is made from cotton, so whenever you can, choose organic to ease the environmental load of all those chemicals.

Or you could try...

If you've ripped an old pair of jeans, why don't you save their life by repairing them with a decorative patch. Use the same technique as the one used here to create pretty patches for repairs.

If you've got a favourite top that you love to wear with your jeans, choose the same colours to make your patch to create a cool, coordinating outfit.

Find your own style

Having the confidence to create your own style with flair is a great skill to have. Fashion trends change with the season, and that's a big part of the reason why fashion can have such a negative effect on the environment. People buy clothes because they're in, then go off them a few months later when something new arrives in the shops.

By learning how to make your own style statement, you'll find you get more out of your clothes and stay on trend by knowing how to revamp, restyle and customise your look.

Trust your taste

Always choose clothes and fabrics in colours and prints that you love. You'll often find these colours naturally go together, making it easier for you to mix and match your wardrobe to create new look after new look.

Dare to experiment

True style icons have never been afraid to step out from the crowd. Throughout time, the real leaders in fashion have always been the first to try new looks and break the mould, rather than staying in line with the fashion herd. If you think something looks good then express your individuality and don't be afraid to show off your inner flair and style!

Revamping, customising and recycling to create new clothes is one of the best ways to express your individuality, because no-one else is going to have that same T-shirt, skirt or scarf. Each item you create will be as individual as you are and be a personal style statement.

Your super slippers would make a great gift!

Look to the future

Today's trend used to be tomorrow's landfill, but by using the projects in this book you can keep your wardrobe fresh without any of the waste.

You could use the techniques in Transfom a T-shirt on page 20 to create a funky skirt or dress, or revamp a bag or top using the techniques in Dazzling Jeans on page 26. You could even make smart felt slippers for your brother or boyfriend using the basic techniques for Slipper Chic on page 24.

The only limits to your style are how far you can stretch your imagination!

Craft skills

How to thread a needle

Cut a length of thread. Make sure it is no longer than your arm; too long a piece of thread will become knotted and make sewing hard work. Pass the tip of the thread through the eye of the needle. If the ends are frayed, dampen them slightly. Hold the two ends of thread together and loop into a knot. Doubling up the thread will help to make your sewing stronger.

Starting and finishing a line of stitching

To start, fasten the thread to the fabric using a few backstitches. End a line of tacking with one backstitch or a knot.

Sewing on buttons

Buttons usually have two or four holes, or have a single loop underneath. They need to be sewn on very firmly with plenty of stitches as they are generally subject to lots of wear and tear.

For a two-hole or looped button, sew through the holes or loop on to the fabric about six times in the same direction.
Tie off on the underside of the fabric.
For a four-hole button, use the same technique as for the two-hole button, using opposite holes to make a cross pattern.

Tacking stitch

This is used to hold the fabric in position while it is being permanently stitched and is ideal for gathering fabric into ruffles. Pass the needle in and out of the fabric in a line to make long, even stitches.

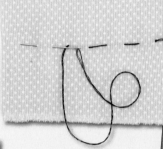

To make ruffles, do not tie off the line of stitching. Gently pull the thread, sliding the fabric together into gathers or ruffles. When you have created the desired effect, tie off with a backstitch or knot.

Running stitch

Similar to the tacking stitch, the running stitch uses smaller stitches. It is used for seams and for gathering and can also be used to decorative effect, particularly with wool or embroidery thread. You can stitch lines or curling patterns onto the surface of fabric.

Pass the needle in and out of the fabric in small, even stitches.

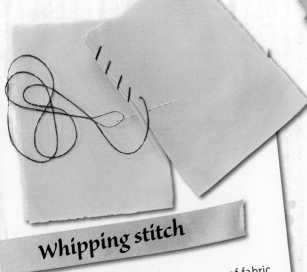

Whipping stitch

This stitch is used to secure two pieces of fabric together at the edges.

Place two pieces of fabric on top of each other.

Fasten the thread to the inside of one piece of fabric. Pass the needle through both pieces of fabric from underneath, passing through where you have fastened the thread. Stitch through from the underside again to make a diagonal stitch about 1 cm from the first stitch.

Blanket stitch

This is a decorative stitch used to bind the edge of fabric. Use a contrasting coloured thread for maximum effect.

Fasten the thread on the underside of the fabric, then pass the needle from the underside. Make a looped stitch over the edge of the fabric but before you pull it tight, pass the needle through the loop. Repeat.

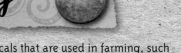
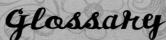

Glossary

Agro-chemicals: chemicals that are used in farming, such as pesticides

Bio-degradable: materials or substances that can be decomposed by natural bacteria

Boho: short for bohemian; someone who is unconventional or artistic

Consumer: a person who buys products and services for personal use

Contaminant: a toxic or poisonous substance that infects or dirties other substances

Decompose: the process by which man-made and natural materials and substances break down. It can be another word for rotting.

Eco: short for ecology; sometimes used in front of words to imply a positive effect on the environment, for example 'eco fashion'

Environment: the natural world, including air, soil, water, plants, and animals

Landfill: also known as a rubbish tip or dump, landfill is a site used for the disposal of waste materials

Organic: plants and animals that are grown or reared entirely naturally without the use of synthetic inputs such as pesticides, fertilizers and antibiotics

Pesticide: a chemical used to prevent, destroy or repel pests

Pollution: the release of environmental contaminants

Recycle: to use something again, usually after processing or remaking in some way

Toxic: poisonous

Trend: popular fashion or style at a given time

Upcycle: to take something that is disposable and transforming it into something of greater use and value

Useful websites

freecycle.org: a website helping to keep unwanted consumer goods out of landfill. It brings together people who want to get rid of things and people who need those things.

ebay.co.uk an auction website where you can bid on other people's unwanted goods and possessions.

etsy.com a website where people can buy and sell handmade crafts. A great source for craft inspiration.

folksy.com a website where people can buy, sell and learn how to make handmade crafts.

recyclethis.co.uk an inspirational website with ideas on how to recycle, reuse and upcycle things that would otherwise go in the bin.

Index